Usborne English Readers

Starter Level

The Rainbow Coat

Retold by Laura Co

Illustrated by Ciara Ní Dhuinn

English language consultant: Peter Viney

Contents

You can listen to the story online here:
usborne.com/rainbowcoataudio

The phoenix is a quiet bird. She has brown feathers and she lives in a tree in the forest. Lots of bird families live in the forest, but they never see the phoenix.

The forest birds are beautiful.
Every bird family is beautiful,
but every one is different.

Some have
long tails and
some have
short ones.

Some have
dark feathers
and some have light ones.

Their feathers are like rainbows,
red, green, yellow, purple and blue.

All day, the forest birds look at
their lovely feathers, sing and
eat food from the trees.

When they are hungry, they can
find food easily. They take berries
from the trees. They eat some.
They give some to their families.

Some berries fall on the ground, and the forest birds forget about them.
The quiet brown phoenix sees the berries on the ground. She picks them up and takes them through the forest to her tree home.

It's always good to have food at home.

Then summer comes. It's a long, hot summer. Every day is hot, and there is no rain.

The trees in the forest have no water. Their leaves change from green to brown. There are no more berries now.

The forest birds try to find food. It
isn't easy. The birds are tired and sad,
and there is no food for their families.
"We're hungry!" sing the birds.
"We're *really* hungry!" sing
their families.

Hungry!

Hungry!

Hungry!

"There's no food. No food!" they sing. "Our families can't eat! What can we do?"

From her tree home, the phoenix hears them.

"I can help," she thinks.

She flies through the forest.

"Come to my house! I have lots of food," she tells the birds.

Come and eat it! Bring your families.

The forest birds fly to the phoenix's home and find all the berries there. There is food for everyone. The forest birds can eat, their families can eat and they are happy.

"Thank you, thank you!" sing the forest birds, "We are so hungry. Our families are so hungry!"

"Eat everything," sings the kind phoenix. "The rain is coming soon. When the rain comes, we can find more berries."

Later, one clever old bird says,
"The phoenix is so good. Can we do
something for her? I know... Please,
everyone, give me one feather."
"Yes, yes, yes!" the birds sing.
Every bird gives a feather.

There are long feathers and short ones, dark feathers and light. The baby birds give little feathers, too. There are red and orange feathers, yellow and green and blue, like a rainbow.

The clever old bird makes a coat with them all, and the birds give it to the phoenix.

This is to say thank you, my friend.

The phoenix is happy. She
loves her rainbow coat, and she has
new friends, too. She isn't brown and
quiet now. She is beautiful and she
is kind, and everyone knows it.

Chinese story animals

The Rainbow Coat is a story from China.

In Chinese stories, the phoenix is black, white, red, gold and blue-green. It is always good and kind.

Another animal in Chinese stories is the dragon. Chinese dragons don't have wings. They are water animals.

At Chinese New Year, you can sometimes see a 'dragon dance'. Lots of dancers carry the dragon between them.

Are there special, magical animals in stories from your country? Which story animals do you like best?

Activities

The answers are on page 24.

Can you see it in the picture?
Which three things *can't* you see?

berries birds coat dragon
feathers forest ground leaves
phoenix sun tail tree

What is the phoenix thinking?

Choose the right words for each picture.

1.

A.
The forest birds need help.

2.

B.
I'm so happy.

3.

C.
I can take this food home.

4.

D.
I don't have any friends.

Beautiful birds

One word in each sentence is wrong.
Can you choose the right one?

1.

Some have long ears
and some have short
ones.

2.

Some have heavy
feathers and some
have light ones.

3.

Your feathers are like
rainbows.

4.

All day they dance and
eat food from the trees.

In the forest

Which of these sentences are true?

1.

The phoenix has lots of friends.

2.

It's a long, hot summer.

3.

The forest birds don't need any food.

4.

The birds give the phoenix a coat.

What are the birds doing?

Choose the right words for each picture.

A. They're listening to the phoenix.
B. They're hungry and they're singing sadly.
C. They're making a coat.
D. They're giving food to their families.

1.

2.

3.

4.

Word list

berries (n pl) small fruits.

fall (v) if something is high up and you let go of it, it falls to the ground.

feathers (n pl) birds have feathers on their wings and their bodies. Their feathers help them to fly.

forest (n) a lot of trees together. Forests are very big. It takes a long time to walk through a forest.

ground (n) the ground is under your feet. You stand and walk on the ground.

hungry (adj) when you don't have enough to eat, you are hungry.

kind (adj) good and nice to other people.

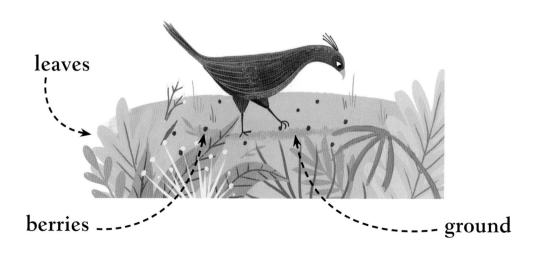

leaves

berries

ground

later (adv) after some time.

leaf, leaves (n) trees and plants have leaves. Leaves are usually green.

phoenix (n) a bird in stories. The phoenix in Chinese stories is beautiful and kind.

rainbow (n) when the sun shines through rain, you sometimes see a rainbow. A rainbow is red, orange, yellow, green, blue and purple.

summer (n) the time of year when it is hot and the sun shines a lot.

through (prep) when you go through a place, for example a town or a forest, you go into the middle of it on your way to somewhere else.

feathers

phoenix

Answers

Can you see it in the picture?

Three things you can't see:
coat, dragon, sun.

What is the phoenix thinking?

1. D
2. C
3. A
4. B

Beautiful birds

1. ~~ears~~ feathers
2. ~~heavy~~ dark
3. ~~Your~~ Their
4. ~~dance~~ sing

In the forest

Sentences 2 and 4 are true.

What are the birds doing?

1. D
2. B
3. A
4. C

 You can find information about other Usborne English Readers here: usborne.com/englishreaders

Designed by Hope Reynolds
Series designer: Laura Nelson Norris
Edited by Mairi Mackinnon

First published in 2021 by Usborne Publishing Ltd.,
Usborne House, 83-85 Saffron Hill, London EC1N 8RT, England.
usborne.com Copyright © 2021 Usborne Publishing Ltd.